Eyes for Evidence

Have You Got What It Takes to Be a Forensic Scientist?

by Lisa Thompson

Compass Point Books ✦ Minneapolis, Minnesota

First American edition published in 2009 by
Compass Point Books
151 Good Counsel Drive
P.O. Box 669
Mankato, MN 56002-0669

Editor: Anthony Wacholtz
Designer: Ashlee Suker
Art Director: LuAnn Ascheman-Adams
Creative Director: Joe Ewest
Editorial Director: Nick Healy
Managing Editor: Catherine Neitge
Content Adviser: Julie A. Heinig, Ph.D.,
              Assistant Laboratory Director of Forensics,
              DNA Diagnostics Center, Fairfield, Ohio

Editor's note: To best explain careers to readers, the author has
created composite characters based on extensive interviews and research.

This book was manufactured with paper containing
at least 10 percent post-consumer waste.

Library of Congress Cataloging-in-Publication Data
Thompson, Lisa.
  Eyes for evidence : have you got what it takes to be a forensic scientist? /
by Lisa Thompson.
     p. cm.—(On the Job)
  Includes index.
  ISBN 978-0-7565-4079-1 (library binding)
  1. Forensic sciences—Juvenile literature. I. Title.
  HV8073.8.M667 2009
  363.25023—dc22   2008038460

Visit Compass Point Books on the Internet at *www.compasspointbooks.com*
or e-mail your request to *custserv@compasspointbooks.com*

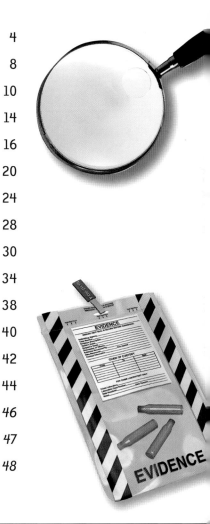

Table of Contents

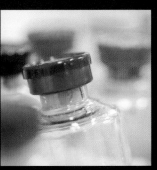

Evidence: The True Witness

It's 8:30 A.M., and I have just arrived at the crime lab. I get a call from Chris Howard, a crime-scene investigator for the lab. He tells me he has just finished collecting evidence from a crime scene—a home invasion and robbery, where a victim was beaten and robbed. The perpetrators fled the scene in a stolen car.

The victim is on the way to the hospital in critical condition. Police are still interviewing witnesses and neighbors. They have some leads but need the help of my team to analyze evidence. The burglars are still at large, so answers are needed quickly.

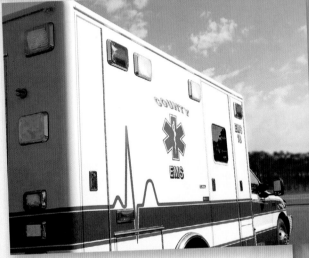

I tell Chris that my team and I will be ready to analyze the evidence as soon as he gets it to the lab.

What is forensic science?

The term forensic relates to anything associated with a court of law, public discussion, or debate. It is more commonly known to the general public as the process of gathering evidence to solve a crime. Forensic science is different from other sciences in that it is the examination of material specifically for use in court.

Forensic science uses many scientific disciplines. Chemical tests; identification of hair, blood, dirt, and cloth fibers; DNA testing; microscopy; forensic psychology; and forensic medicine are just a few of the many branches of science used in the analysis of evidence.

A forensic scientist may specialize in the following fields:

forensic anthropology—the identification of skeletal human remains

forensic entomology—the examination of insects on and around human remains; used to help identify the time and location of death

forensic biology—DNA analysis of bodily fluids, teeth, hair, bone, and tissue to identify a person

forensic odontology—the study of teeth; used to identify the victim

forensic toxicology—the study of the effect of drugs and poisons on and in the human body

forensic geology—the study of trace evidence, such as soils, minerals, and petroleum

forensic psychology—the study of a person's mind, usually to determine reasons behind a criminal's behavior

forensic trace evidence—the study of hairs, fibers, paint chips, gunshot residue, fingerprints, trace metal detection, and tire prints

Forensic geology

The work of a forensic scientist can be divided into three areas:

Field work—collecting the evidence at a crime scene

Laboratory work—analyzing the evidence

Court work—presenting the evidence, including reporting the findings from the lab work, preparing documents for court or for other scientists, and testifying in court

Fibers under a microscope

A forensic scientist may perform the following tasks:

- identify illegal drugs
- analyze drugs and poisons in human tissue and body fluids, including blood-alcohol levels
- examine and compare materials such as fibers, paints, cosmetics, oils, gasoline, plastics, glass, metals, soils, and gunshot residues
- conduct DNA profiling
- perform document examinations
- examine crime scenes
- identify firearms and ammunition
- detect and identify fingerprints, footprints, and tool marks
- analyze tire marks and tracks
- conduct botanical identification
- examine fire and explosion scenes for the origin and cause
- prepare evidence reports for court
- advise police investigators, scientists, and pathologists

Why I Became a Forensic Scientist

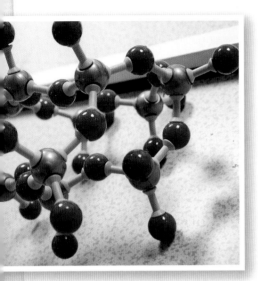

When I was in school, I developed a passion for science, especially chemistry and biology. I really enjoyed the process of finding answers and solving problems in the science laboratory.

After high school I went to college to study biology and chemistry. While there I was able to get some work experience in an actual crime lab. The lab environment made science even more exciting and interesting.

People always ask me if it is hard to remain objective, especially if I am working on a high-profile case. I don't think it's hard because forensic science is about the scientific analysis of evidence. It is not about who is involved in the case.

Evidence has a way of surprising you—when analyzed correctly, it cannot lie. I love putting the pieces of evidence together to help solve a case. With advances in forensic science, such as DNA profiling, we are getting faster at understanding the evidence we find. We are also developing better, more accurate methods of analysis. All of this keeps the job exciting for me!

Traits needed for forensic science:

- good communication skills
- ability to remain unbiased when examining evidence
- attention to detail
- skilled at clear, logical thinking
- ability to work as part of a team
- self-motivation
- persistence
- good observational skills

Forensic Science Through History

In ancient Rome a criminal charge meant presenting the case before a group of people. Both the person accused of the crime and the accuser gave speeches based on their sides of the story. The person with the best argument and delivery determined the outcome of the case.

Chinese forensics

The book *Xi Yuan Ji Lu* (*Collected Cases of Injustice Rectified*), written by Chinese author Song Ci in 1248, contains one of the earliest written accounts of using medicine and entomology to solve criminal cases. A death investigator solved a case of a person murdered with a sickle. He asked everyone to bring their sickles to the same location. Flies, attracted by the smell of blood, eventually gathered on one sickle. From this evidence, the murderer confessed.

19th-century blood tests

Until the 1900s, scientists could not effectively examine dried blood under a microscope. They could not identify blood types or even distinguish between human blood and animal blood.

Fingerprint designs

In 1892, Sir Francis Galton wrote *Fingerprints*, a book about how prints could help solve crimes. Galton figured out the first system for classifying fingerprints. The Galton-Henry system was officially introduced at Scotland Yard in 1901 and quickly became the basis for identification records. His book changed forensic science forever.

Who Inspired Sherlock Holmes?

Sir Arthur Conan Doyle

Sherlock Holmes is the fictional character Sir Arthur Conan Doyle created in works he wrote from 1887 to 1915. Conan Doyle based the character of Sherlock Holmes on his teacher, the gifted surgeon and forensic detective Joseph Bell.

Bell was renowned for being observant. He emphasized the importance of close observation when making a diagnosis. He was even able to deduce the occupation and recent activities of a stranger on the street, simply by observing him.

Illustrations from **The Adventures of Sherlock Holmes, 1892–1893**

Edmond Locard (1877–1966)

Edmond Locard was a pioneer in forensic science and became known as the Sherlock Holmes of France. He was an assistant to Alexandre Lacassagne, a professor of forensic medicine at the University of Lyon. Locard formulated the basic principle of forensic science —every contact leaves a trace. This is known as Locard's exchange principle.

In 1910, Locard started his own criminal laboratory. He produced a monumental seven-volume work, Traite de Criminalistique. In 1918, he developed 12 matching points for fingerprint identification. He continued his research until his death in 1966.

Caught red-handed

In 1902, Henry "Harry" Jackson was the first person in the United Kingdom convicted on fingerprint evidence. He was a burglar who placed his hands in wet paint during a robbery, thus leaving behind his fingerprints. Can you guess his crime? Jackson stole billiard balls!

The Crime Scene

Every crime scene is unique. It is important that police seal off the area as quickly as possible to preserve any potential evidence. The crime-scene investigators arrive soon after the police and detectives to process the crime scene. People sometimes contaminate evidence by touching things and walking around. Evidence can also disappear shortly after a crime because of weather or environmental changes.

CRIME SCENE

POLICE LINE DO NOT CROSS   POLICE LINE

Police mark off the crime scene.

The forensic photographer at work

Crime fighting on TV

Television and movies tend to focus on murder cases, but in reality, only about 1 percent of a typical forensic laboratory workload involves homicides. Drugs, robbery, and fraud are more common areas of investigation, with drunk driving topping the list.

Documenting crime

The main ways to document crime scenes are through clearly written notes, sketches, and photographs, and by recording evidence on video.

A crime-scene investigator searches for evidence.

Crime-scene notes should include the following information:

- date and time the police were called
- address of the crime and a description of the area
- name of the person who called the crime-scene investigator
- names of all the people present at the crime scene, including those who took photographs and fingerprints
- weather and lighting conditions
- descriptions and locations of any bodies found
- locations of all evidence found
- descriptions of the interior and exterior of the crime scene
- date and time the crime-scene investigation was finished

Investigators must have as little physical contact as possible with evidence as they tag, bag, and record it. It is important to leave any material that is collected in its original state.

Evidence

The study of physical evidence is the basis of forensic science. Trace evidence is material found at a crime or accident scene in small but measurable amounts. The study of trace evidence relies on Locard's exchange principle—that every contact, no matter how slight, will leave a trace. Forensic scientists should always wear disposable gloves at a crime scene to make sure they don't contaminate the evidence.

Principles behind gathering trace evidence:

1 Every contact between two people or between a person and an object leaves evidence on both.

2 Trace evidence that is found, documented, and examined can link a person to a specific time and/or place.

3 Individual characteristics, physical matches, and mathematical probability all help identify trace evidence.

Sniffing out evidence

Some evidence at a crime scene is invisible, such as the scent left behind by people, drugs, or explosive products. With their excellent sense of smell, specially trained dogs can sniff out even the weakest scents. They can also detect human remains and tell the difference between new and older scents.

Crime-scene investigators may also use a machine that sucks up smells on a scent pad. These scents from the crime scene can be freeze-dried and given to a sniffer dog later to match the scent to a suspect or other evidence.

Physical evidence is any object that:

- establishes a crime has been committed
- provides a link between a crime and the victim
- provides a link between a crime and the suspect

Types of physical evidence:

- blood and saliva
- documents
- drugs
- explosives
- fingerprints
- firearms, ammunition, and gunshot residue
- glass
- hairs and fibers
- insects
- paint chips
- soils
- tool marks and impressions
- tracks or markings

Hair fibers may link a suspect to a crime.

20 ml

A Chain of Custody

After collecting the evidence, it is crucial that the material remains in its original condition. To preserve evidence, investigators follow certain pro-cedures to maintain a chain of custody. The name of the collecting official and his or her signature are recorded, as well as the date and time the evidence was collected. The location where the evidence was found is also noted.

Collecting evidence

When sealing the evidence, special tamper-evident seals are used. These seals make it easy to see if the evidence has been altered. Both recording who had possession of the evidence and sealing the evidence properly are critical to proving the evidence's reliability.

Tests are conducted at the lab.

Forensic photography

Forensic photography is one part of the evidence-collecting process. Photos are also useful in court because they can visually depict important aspects of the crime scene.

Forensic photography involves choosing correct lighting so images are as clear and precise as possible. The accurate angling of the camera lens and a collection of various viewpoints are also important. Pictures should include scales or rulers to accurately record the dimensions of the crime scene evidence.

3-D crime fighting

A company in Toronto, Canada, called MDRobotics has developed the Instant Scene Modeler—a video camera that can record crime scenes. From the data recorded, a computer generates a 3-D reconstruction of the crime scene so that investigators can measure items from the crime scene. They can also play out scenarios without tampering with evidence. The Instant Scene Modeler can visually recreate crime scenes for juries and lawyers in a courtroom.

Fingerprints

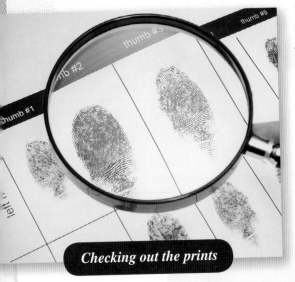

Checking out the prints

Fingerprint analysis is probably the most well-known use of forensic science. In the past police would spend hours trying to manually match fingerprints to a set in their records. Today computers can compare one set of fingerprints against half a million others in less than a second.

Once the computer identifies potential matches, two forensic scientists compare the prints separately.

Dacty-what?

The study of fingerprints is called dactyloscopy. It comes from the Greek words *daktylos*, meaning "finger," and *skopein*, meaning "to examine."

What pattern do you have?

There are four main patterns of fingerprints:

- Loops—About 60 percent of fingerprints have loops, which have a stronger curve than arches.

- Whorls—About 30 percent of fingerprints form a complete oval, often in a spiral pattern.

- Arches—About 5 percent of people have arches, which are formed by ridges running across the finger.

- The fourth pattern is a mixture of the other three patterns.

Each fingertip has a pattern of fine skin ridges that are slightly different for each person, even identical twins. Whenever you touch something, you leave behind a faint smear of grease, dust, or sweat. The unique pattern on your fingers stays on everything you touch.

Evidence is everywhere if you look closely enough.

Lifting Fingerprints

The most common technique for lifting fingerprints is dusting a surface with a very fine powder and a brush. The powder sticks to the oils deposited by fingertips and outlines the ridge details of the prints. The powder prints are then placed onto tape, which is attached to a card and sealed in an evidence bag.

Various light wavelengths are often used to detect fingerprints. For example, ultraviolet (UV) light is commonly used to uncover fingerprints after an investigator brushes a surface with fluorescent powder. The powder sticks to the prints and shows up under the UV light. A wide range of chemical treatments can also detect fingerprints.

Laser scanning

A laser scanning procedure can record fingerprints by placing the hand on a flat, glass plate. The print is then stored in a computer and compared to other prints electronically.

Not 100 percent accurate

Fingerprint evidence can be subjective and depends on the expert. There have been several cases throughout history and around the globe where convictions were made purely on the basis of fingerprint evidence—but the expert turned out to be wrong.

One instance of a reversed outcome happened in Portland, Oregon, in 2004. Brandon Mayfield was arrested for bombing a train in Madrid, Spain, and the FBI determined that his fingerprints were found at the scene of the crime. Investigators from Spain were not convinced that the fingerprints matched those of Mayfield, and they later found a more likely suspect. Mayfield was then released.

Bloodstains

Blood, as well as other body fluids found at a crime scene, may contain crucial physical evidence.

- A bloodstain on either an object or at a location may prove that a weapon was used or that a crime has taken place.
- Shape, position, size, or intensity of a bloodstain may support a particular theory of how and when certain events occurred.
- Analysis of DNA from the blood can eliminate groups of people as suspects.

Blood types

In 1901, scientists found that there are four main human blood groups: A, B, AB, and O. Types A and O are the most common groups, and type AB is the rarest. Within these types, a person's blood can be positive or negative (known as the Rhesus factor). The Rhesus factor type is written after the ABO type, such as A+ or O-. Since 1950 scientists have also known how to determine whether blood came from a male or female.

Blood-pattern analysis

Blood-pattern analysis is the study of blood patterns. The type of blood pattern can reveal many things about a crime—where the crime occurred, the number of attackers, and the type of weapon used.

Pools of blood or smears around a body show whether the body was dragged. The angle the blood hits a surface can reveal the direction of the attack. The distance between blood drops and how far they have spattered can sometimes indicate where an attack took place and how the attack happened.

Blood spatter

Pool of blood

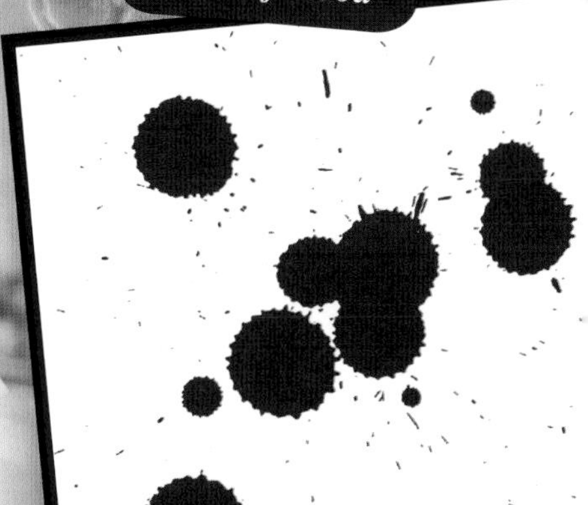

Blood droplets

Analyzing blood under a microscope

Blood Clues

It is very important that investigators consider the size and shape of bloodstains. They also need to analyze the surface the blood hits because different surfaces will cause different spatter patterns. The harder the surface, the less the blood will spatter. After a blood drop hits a surface, its shape will either be round or elliptical, which helps determine the direction from which it came.

A drop of blood

A drop of blood is normally a sphere or ball-shaped, not the common teardrop shape often depicted. A typical blood drop is about .002 ounces (.05 milliliters).

The luminol test

It is important for forensic scientists to locate weak or invisible stains, any of which may contain valuable evidence. Although the luminol test cannot conclusively prove stains are blood, it can light up invisible stains with a blue light. This test is sensitive enough to pick up minute traces, even when someone has tried to wash them away. Other types of light can detect the fluorescence of body fluids like saliva or sweat.

Clotting

The time that blood takes to clot and dry can often indicate when an offense was committed. Blood, after leaving the body, usually takes between three and six minutes to clot.

DNA Analysis

DNA is a chemical containing the instructions for making the structures the body needs to function. Besides red blood cells, all human cells have DNA. Every person is unique—no two people have the same DNA, unless they are identical twins.

DNA profiling helps police identify an individual. The process of DNA profiling involves comparing DNA samples to determine whether they could be from the same person.

DNA can be extracted from any bodily fluid, such as blood, saliva, or sweat. DNA can also be found in hair roots and skin.

Skin cells under a microscope

The Innocence Project

The Innocence Project uses DNA profiling to check evidence that may have wrongly convicted a person of murder. The Innocence Project has resulted in the pardon of more than 200 innocent people who had been sent to prison.

DNA on fingerprints

In the past DNA analysis was restricted to samples of blood, tissue, or bodily fluids. Then, in 1996, an Australian team of scientists was the first to prove that DNA can be analyzed from the few skin cells left behind on fingerprints. These few cells can provide forensic scientists with a complete DNA profile.

A smudged fingerprint may contain DNA.

Broken glass may offer helpful clues.

Broken glass

Glass is often broken during a crime, and tiny fragments are commonly caught in clothing. They can remain hidden even if the suspect washes the clothes many times. If the fragments are recovered from the clothing, forensic scientists can analyze them to determine whether they match the glass broken at the crime scene.

Forensic Bugs

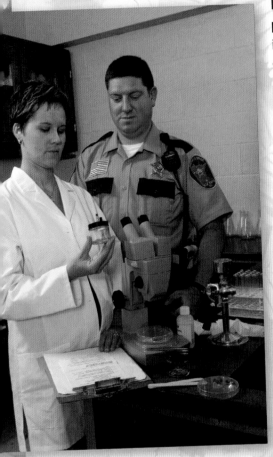

Insects on a corpse often provide clues that help identify the circumstances surrounding the death. They can help determine the time of death, the location of wounds, whether a body has been moved, and even if drugs were present in the body at the time of death.

Evidence in insects

If an insect has fed on a victim, forensic entomologists are able to test the human DNA found in an insect's intestines, possibly matching a corpse to a missing person. Or if an insect has fed on both the victim and the suspect, the DNA can possibly make a connection between the two individuals.

Time of death

Forensic entomologists study the life cycle of maggots and flies to help calculate a victim's time of death. Flies quickly discover a dead body and begin to lay eggs that develop into maggots.

PUN FUN
Forensic scientists are often in grave situations.

Forensic entomologists also look at the temperature and environmental conditions of the crime scene. Weather conditions will affect the size and development of the eggs and larvae on a corpse.

Maggots

The maggot is the main feeding stage of a fly. On hatching, larvae are less than 1/10 inch (2 millimeters) long, growing to about 1/5 inch (5 mm) before shedding their skin. The second stage larvae grow to around 2/5 inch (10 mm), and the third stage grow to between 3/5 and 4/5 inch (15 and 20 mm). A maggot can grow from 1/10 inch to 4/5 inch in four days. It then becomes a pupa before transforming into a fly.

Undercover Bugs

Maggot masses

Maggots travel around in maggot masses. Their digestive activities are so intense that the corpse heats up under a maggot mass, sometimes reaching 127 degrees Fahrenheit (53 degrees Celsius).

The heat increases the maggots' rate of digestion. It can get so hot inside a maggot mass that maggots at the center of a body have to move to the edge of the body to cool down.

Maggots also reveal secret information contained within the body, such as whether the body contained drugs at the time of death. If a person was under the influence of drugs before death, the maggots collect the drugs from the flesh they have eaten. By testing the maggots, scientists can identify the drugs.

Bugs on the move

Bugs on a body may also indicate that a body has been moved because different surroundings contain different bugs. If someone moved a body after a crime, the insects on the body would not match the surroundings. Moving a body after bugs have arrived can also disturb the insects' life cycles, alerting forensic entomologists of a move.

The body farm

The University of Tennessee Forensic Anthropology Facility has a body farm where scientists study human decomposition after death. It consists of a 3-acre (1.2-hectare) wooded plot surrounded by a razor wire fence and contains a number of bodies scattered throughout the area. More than 300 people have voluntarily donated their bodies to the body farm. The bodies are exposed in various ways to show how they decompose under various conditions, such as in shallow graves, car trunks, entombed vaults, or an open area.

Document Analysis

By carefully studying documents, investigators may be able to determine a likely suspect or motive.

Examiners use various methods to analyze a document, starting with direct visual examination. They may use magnifying lenses, microscopes, and devices that use infrared and UV lights. The paper and ink of a document can also be chemically analyzed.

Document inspection under lights

Preparing the evidence

Documents that are ready for analysis are placed in thin, clear plastic folders so the items are protected. They are then marked as exhibits, given a reference number, and photographed.

COLD CASE #00254-8774

Dating documents

Forensic scientists can date a document by analyzing the materials used in a document, such as inks and dyes. This technique is useful but limited. Depending on the ink used, the test can only determine whether a document was produced before or after 1950.

PUN FUN

Nap time! Police brought a 3-year-old child to the police station for resisting a rest.

Handwritten Versus Printed Documents

All document evidence can be broken down into two main categories—handwritten documents and printed documents. Analyzing handwritten documents may help to expose forgeries, confirm that a document is genuine, or identify who wrote the document.

Handwritten signatures

Examiners will compare a signature in question to genuine samples of a person's signature. They will then compare the rhythm and flow of the writing.

SIGNATURE

Often suspects or victims are required to provide samples of their handwriting. Most right-handed people tend to write with a slant so that the top of the letters point to the upper right, and the bottom of the letters point to the lower left. The opposite is true for left-handed people. A right-handed person would find it difficult to forge a left-handed person's writing, and vice versa.

Printed documents

In 2005, scientists discovered that some inkjet and laser printers applied a small series of yellow dots to all pages during the printing process. These yellow dots, when viewed through a microscope and decoded, indicated the serial number of the printer, as well as the date and time of the printout. Forensic scientists can trace the serial numbers back to retail sales and individuals, leading to many successes in uncovering illegal printing and counterfeiting.

Tool Markings and Impressions

Tool-mark analysis deals with the impressions or damage made by tools used in a crime. Firearm analysis, for example, determines if a bullet or cartridge came from a particular gun. Empty cartridge casings are the most common items of evidence encountered at the scene of a shooting. Markings that cover a spent cartridge can identify the type of firearm used. If the shooter handled the bullets, fingerprint traces may be present on the cartridge casings. Loading, firing, and reloading a weapon can also make impressions on a firearm.

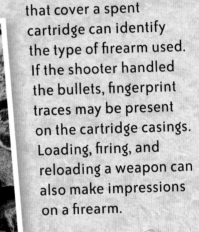

Eyewitness testimony

Physical evidence is more reliable than eyewitness testimony. Experiments have shown that observations made by people witnessing a simulated crime become increasingly inaccurate over a period of time.

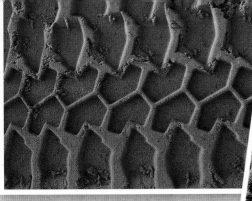

Impression markings

Impression evidence, such as shoe prints or tire marks, are photographed at the scene of the crime. Sometimes molds are made so the original item can be identified. Shoe prints can reveal a person's height and weight, while tire marks may indicate the make and model of the vehicle.

Forensic footprints

Footprints may reveal not only what type of shoes suspects wore, but also their likely age, the direction they took, how fast they were going, and even if they were carrying anything.

PUN FUN
The hostage couldn't stay on the phone long because he was tied up at the moment.

Back at the Lab

When the evidence arrives at the lab, a number of teams, including mine, begin to analyze the material. Everyone on the team must wear gloves, a mask, and a disposable lab coat when working with the evidence. As more tests are completed, facts begin to emerge from our findings.

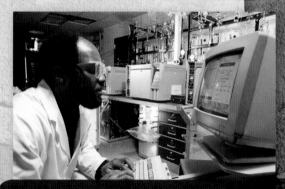

Back at the lab, our team makes some interesting discoveries.

Fingerprints

Tests on fingerprint samples reveal there were at least three people who broke into the house and attacked the victim. Two sets of fingerprints match those found in the police system. Both people have prior records for assault and robbery.

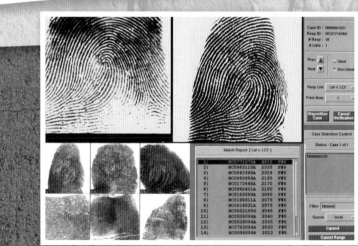

Tool markings

Markings found on the front door indicate that the intruders forced their way into the victim's house. Tests show that the markings match those made by a crowbar.

Document analysis

A number of threatening letters were scattered over the crime scene. Further analysis identified signature forgeries on a few of them.

Impressions

A series of shoe prints found on the carpet at the crime scene are tested and cross-checked.

Blood and DNA analysis

Blood at the crime scene is a match to the victim's. It is cross-checked with other spatters found, including those on a vase and on a piece of wood from the front yard.

Trace evidence

Tests on paint and soil samples found near shoe prints at the crime scene indicate that one of the intruders had worn shoes near sand recently. Another pair of shoes had left traces of paint behind. Hair fibers found at the scene are also analyzed.

What the Evidence Suggests

From our analysis, police narrowed the field of suspects. We concluded from the DNA, fingerprint, and trace-evidence tests that a group of at least three people participated in the attack and robbery.

After further investigation, police discovered that one of the intruders lives near the beach, accounting for the sand in the shoe prints. Another was a house painter, explaining the traces of paint left behind.

In the end, with the help of our lab results, police charged four men and recovered the stolen money and jewelry.

No evidence

The absence of evidence can sometimes be as helpful as having evidence. This theory is useful when trying to disprove the story of a victim or suspect. For example, a victim may claim that his or her shirt was cut with a knife during a fight. After examining the shirt, investigators might find that the shirt was not cut, but torn. The absence of cutting damage would help disprove the victim's claim of being assaulted with a knife.

Forensic science on TV

TV makes evidence analysis appear to be fast and simple, when in reality, crime labs can take weeks or months to analyze and process evidence. Certain chemical processes can take days, and if a piece of evidence has to go through several chemical tests, the process takes even longer.

TV crime shows take the job descriptions of approximately five different forensic specialists and combine them into one "super scientist." This person conducts any type of analysis, almost entirely on his or her own. In reality, a forensics laboratory consists of at least six sections, where many forensic specialists each analyze one piece of evidence before deciding if the evidence reveals something.

My team and I compiled our findings as police reports for use in court. On this occasion, I am required to present DNA profiling evidence of the four accused men in court. More often, I am not required to attend a hearing in person. My findings are just submitted to the court as evidence.

A major part of my job is explaining scientific results. We frequently need to clarify our findings for those who have no scientific knowledge, such as police officers, lawyers, and jury members. It is crucial that we don't use scientific jargon when preparing documents.

Job Opportunities

Follow these steps to become a forensic scientist

Step 1

Study a variety of science subjects at school, especially chemistry, biology, and physics.

Step 2

Complete a college degree specializing in forensic science.

Step 3

Consider taking postgraduate courses related to forensic science.

Step 4

Get hands-on experience in a lab or at a crime scene with professionals. Practicing public speaking so you can clearly express yourself when giving evidence in court will also help.

Step 5

Think about whether you'd like to work in a lab or out in the field. Forensic scientists generally work in one or the other.

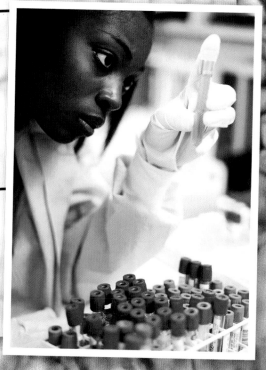

Opportunities for forensic scientists

Forensic science is a highly competitive field. Most forensic science positions are with law enforcement agencies.

Forensic scientists can work in a variety of areas:

- crime-scene examinations
- fingerprint identification
- firearms and ammunition identification
- document examination
- forensic biology
- forensic chemistry
- computer forensics

Other industries that employ forensic scientists:

- Fire investigation units—investigate how fires start and how they spread; their discoveries can convict arsonists

- State chemistry labs—assist government agencies in their investigations, concentrating on drug, fingerprint, or document analysis

- Occupational Safety and Health Administration (OSHA)— investigate the cause of accidents in the workplace, such as whether a manufacturer produced faulty machinery

- Private laboratories—work primarily on nongovernment-related legal issues, such as paternity testing in family law disputes

- Insurance agencies—primarily investigate fires to determine whether they were ignited on purpose or by accident

A career in forensic science is extremely satisfying and rewarding. Few professions offer such an exciting, interesting, and fulfilling career.

Find Out More

In the Know

- More often than not, evidence in a crime scene is not found during the first inspection. Investigators usually analyze a crime scene several times.
- The murder rate portrayed on forensic science TV shows is about 1,000 times higher than in real life.
- Professional journals, such as the *Journal of Forensic Science* and *Forensic Science Communications*, provide forensic experts with the latest news and technologies in the field.
- As of May 2007, the U.S. Department of Labor estimates that the average hourly wage for a forensic science technician is $24.19, equaling $50,310 a year. The lowest 10 percent earned $21,790, and the highest 10 percent earned more than $76,440.

Further Reading

Cooper, Chris. *Forensic Science*. New York: DK Publishing, 2008.

Fridell, Ron. *Forensic Science*. Minneapolis: Lerner Publications, 2007.

Platt, Richard. *Forensics*. Boston: Kingfisher, 2005.

Rainis, Kenneth G. *Forgery: Crime-Solving Experiments*. Berkeley Heights, N.J.: Enslow Publishers, 2006.

On the Web

For more information on this topic, use FactHound.
1. Go to *www.facthound.com*
2. Choose your grade level.
3. Begin your search.
This book's ID number is 9780756540791
FactHound will find the best sites for you.

Glossary

arsonists—people who deliberately set fire to something

assault—violent attack on someone

botanical—referring to the scientific study of plants

cartridge—tube containing a bullet and an explosive substance; used in guns

convictions—when people are found to be guilty in a court of law

counterfeit—something made to look genuine, in order to deceive people

dactyloscopy—study of fingerprints

DNA profiling—process of comparing DNA samples to determine if they are from the same person

entomology—study of insects

follicles—small sacs or cavities in the body, such as for hair

fraud—something that deceives people in an illegal or immoral way

homicide—crime of murder

jargon—words that are used in special or technical ways by particular groups

microscopy—an investigation, observation, or experiment that involves the use of a microscope

odontology—study of teeth

pathologists—doctors or scientists who study the nature and cause of disease

perpetrators—people who commit a certain act, such as a crime

sickle—short-handled tool with a curved blade; used for cutting tall grass or grain

specialists—people who have a particular skill or who know a lot about a particular subject

tampering—interfering with or damaging something

toxicology—study of the effect of drugs and poisons on or in the human body

vaults—strong, secure rooms where valuables are stored; burial chambers

Index

Look for More Books in This Series: